SCHOOL BUS

Were Early Computers Really the Size of a School Bus?

And Other Questions about Inventions

DEBORAH KOPS

ILLUSTRATIONS BY COLIN W. THOMPSON

LERNER PUBLICATIONS COMPANY

Minneapolis

Contents

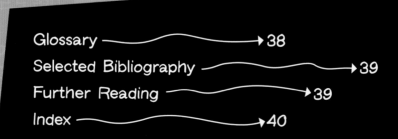

Perhaps you've heard beliefs like these about inventions:

Early computers were the size of a school bus! Henry Ford invented the automobile!

But are these beliefs true? Is there anything to the stories you've heard? Come along with us as we explore the world of inventions. Find out whether our perceptions about inventions are

FACT OR **FICTION!**

Was Gutenberg's Bible the First Printed Book?

NO. The famous Gutenberg Bible *(below)*, printed in 1455, was the first book printed with movable metal type. But it wasn't the first printed book.

People had been printing books in China since the 800s. Instead of using movable letters, they carved the sentences of one page at a time into wood or a soft metal. Then that page could be printed on paper many times for multiple copies of a book.

But Europeans didn't know how to print books. They copied books by hand until the 1400s. Hand-copying was slow and often led to errors. Johannes Gutenberg found a faster, better way to print books—with movable metal type and his printing press.

Gutenberg made many copies of each letter of the alphabet in metal. Then he arranged the letters into sentences in his printing press. This press had once been used for squeezing juice from grapes! Gutenberg spread ink over the letters, put a sheet of paper on top, and used the machine to press the paper against the letters. He could print many copies of a page this way. When he was done, he rearranged the letters so he could print the pages that came next.

With Gutenberg's new printing method, Europeans began printing books like crazy! Only fifty years after Gutenberg printed the Bible, there were about ten million printed books in Europe.

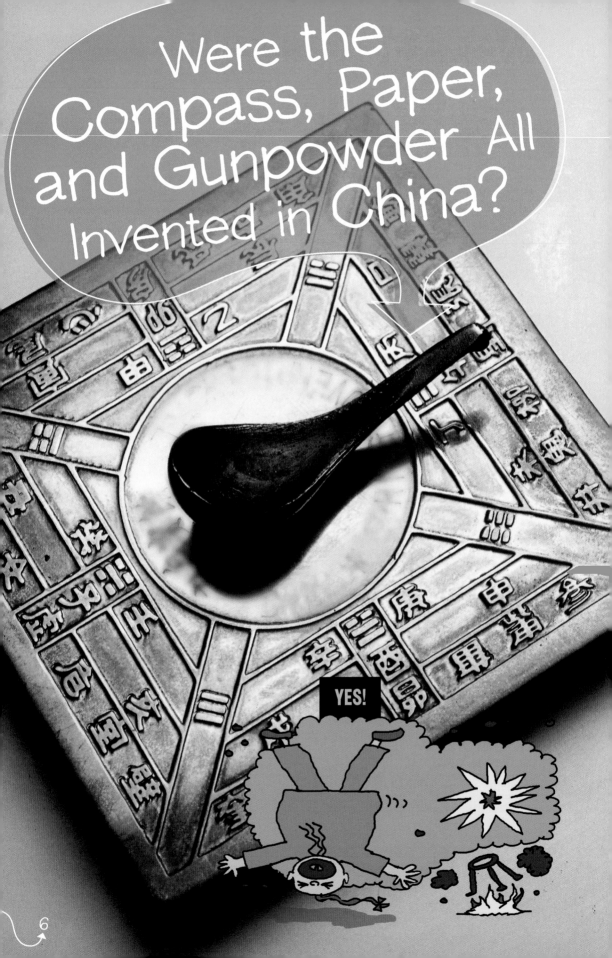

Were the Compass, Paper, and Gunpowder All Invented in China?

YES!

Chinese people were using paper and gunpowder hundreds of years before Europeans. And the Chinese began making compasses *(opposite page)* at least a thousand years sooner. These early compasses were actually rocks that contained lots of magnetite. Magnetite is a mineral. Rocks that contain large amounts of it act like magnets. The Chinese began using these rocks in about 300 B.C. to discover which directions were north and south for spiritual practices. The Chinese did not yet use their compasses for travel.

slowly spread across Asia. By 770, the Japanese were making paper too.

Like many inventions, gunpowder was discovered by accident. Around A.D. 850, Chinese alchemists, or early scientists, were trying to find a way to live forever. One alchemist heated a powdered mixture that exploded. No one knows who that alchemist was. But he had discovered a way to bring death instead of never-ending life.

Drying paper fibers in ancient China

Did You Know?
The old Chinese recipe for making gunpowder is still used in modern times. But it isn't used to make ammunition. Instead, it's used to make something you may have thought was all American: fireworks! Gunpowder is the main ingredient in those dazzling explosions that you see on the Fourth of July.

In about A.D. 100, the Chinese figured out how to make paper. They used all sorts of things to make paper, including bark, bamboo, and sometimes rags. First, they pounded the substance in water. Then they poured the watery mixture through some loosely woven cloth. The fibers that remained on top of the cloth dried and formed paper. News of how the Chinese made paper

Did Leonardo da Vinci Really Come Up with a Design for a Helicopter?

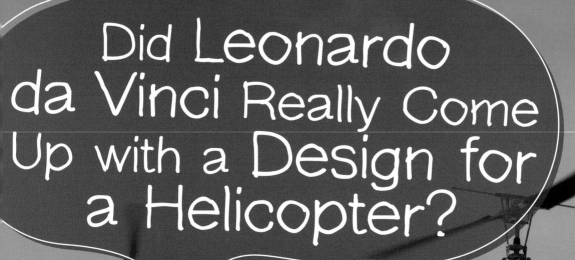

YES. Leonardo da Vinci (1452–1519) is best known for his famous painting the *Mona Lisa*. But this Italian artist was also an engineer. Around 1480, he produced the earliest known design for a helicopter. On top sat a giant screw. Leonardo thought that if the screw whirled around fast enough, the aircraft would rise. But his helicopter needed a source of power. There were no engines back in the 1400s. So Leonardo's design could not work.

Leonardo da Vinci

A sketch of da Vinci's helicopter

Igor Sikorsky flies a helicopter he designed. It was the first successful helicopter.

In the 1860s, a Frenchman by the name of Gustave Ponton d'Amecourt built small model helicopters. Some were powered by steam engines. But they didn't work very well. A model that shot up into the air with the help of a spring worked better. Later attempts at designing a helicopter included one by George de Bothezat. He built a helicopter for the U.S. Army in 1922 with a gasoline engine. It was nicknamed the flying octopus and flew close to the ground. In 1939 the Russian-born Igor Sikorsky designed the first successful helicopter. It operated like a modern helicopter.

A modern helicopter gets its lift from its blades, which rotate like the blades on a ceiling fan. These are called the rotor. The rotor lets a helicopter rise straight up from the ground. It also allows the helicopter to hover like a hummingbird or a bee. It works very much as da Vinci imagined.

Thousands of years before da Vinci dreamed up his helicopter, Chinese children played with a toy that resembled helicopters. It was simply a few feathers on the end of a stick. The child spun the stick in his or her hands and tossed it in the air. Where did that idea come from? The inspiration may have been the blade-shaped seedpod from a sycamore tree, whirling in the breeze.

Is It True That Galileo Invented the Telescope?

NOPE. In 1609, Galileo became the first person to use a telescope to study the night sky. The telescope was still a new invention, but Galileo wasn't the inventor. No one is sure who invented the telescope. One of the most likely people was Hans Lippershey.

Hans Lippershey in about 1600

Lippershey made eyeglasses for people in the Dutch Republic (modern-day Netherlands). In the early 1600s, he decided to make an instrument. It would make something in the distance appear to be much closer. He put a curved piece of glass on one end of a tube. On the other end, he put another curved piece of glass. The curve on each piece of glass faced in the opposite direction. The glass refracted, or bent, light as it passed through the glass, making objects appear closer. Lippershey had built a refracting telescope.

In 1608, Lippershey applied for a patent for his invention. Patents allow only the person who came up with an invention to make and sell that invention. But at least two other men claimed they invented the telescope. So no one got the patent.

About sixty years later, the Englishman Isaac Newton introduced a different design for a telescope. He put two mirrors in the telescope. Working together, the mirrors allowed the viewer to see a sharp reflection of an object. Newton had built the first reflecting telescope.

The telescope on the right is a reflecting telescope like the one Isaac Newton used. The telescope on the left is a refracting telescope like Lippershey's.

Galileo made some important discoveries with his refracting telescope. In 1610, he discovered that Jupiter had four moons. A year later, he noticed that the dark spots he saw on the sun seemed to move. Galileo realized the sun was rotating on its axis (an imaginary line through the middle of an object, around which the object spins). After studying outer space for decades, Galileo decided that Earth and other planets moved around the sun. This was not a new idea. But it made the Roman Catholic Church angry. At the time, the church claimed that Earth was the center of the universe. When Galileo published his beliefs in a book, church officials arrested him.

Modern astronomers still use refracting telescopes like Lippershey's and Galileo's for looking at the moon and the planets. But they use reflecting telescopes to study objects that are farther away, such as stars.

Did Benjamin Franklin Invent the Lightning Rod?

YES. Franklin discovered that a metal rod in a high spot attracted lightning. And he figured out what would happen if the rod stood on the roof of a building and was connected to the ground by a wire. If lightning struck the building, the rod would conduct (carry) the electrical charge from the lightning to the ground. And the building would be safe. Without the rod, a lightning strike could set a building on fire and hurt people.

Did You Know?

Electricity fascinated people in the middle of the eighteenth century. In Britain and colonial America, people gave electricity parties. They entertained their guests by using electric charges to ring bells, make wires jump, and move fake spiders.

By the fall of 1752, Franklin had put a lightning rod atop the Pennsylvania State House in Philadelphia. He also put one on his own house. In his publication *Poor Richard's Almanac*, he told his readers how to install their own lightning rods.

Just a few months before Franklin put up the lightning rods, he had made a major discovery. He had proved to scientists in Europe and colonial America that lightning was a form of electricity. At the time, many people thought lightning was a frightening mystery or a punishment from God. Franklin had showed that lightning was natural. And he knew lightning would be even less scary if people could protect themselves and their homes from dangerous lightning strikes.

Ben Franklin flew a kite during a thunderstorm to prove that lightning is a form of electricity. He succeeded, capturing the lightning's charge in a jar connected to the kite. But he was lucky to survive. The electric charge could easily have killed him!

Did Two Papermakers Really Invent the Hot-Air Balloon?

PROBABLY. The earliest balloon flight ever recorded occurred in the French town of Annonay in June 1783. Two brothers, Joseph and Jacques Montgolfier, had made the balloon. And the Mongolfier brothers did make paper for a living. The year before that balloon flight, they had made a discovery. When they directed hot air from a fire into a bag made out of silk, the bag rose in the air.

Jacques and Joseph Montgolfier

On that June morning, people gathered around the town square to watch the Montgolfiers' balloon. At first, it looked like a big pile of silk. It was 35 feet (10 meters) wide and weighed about 500 pounds (227 kilograms). At the opening of the balloon, the brothers attached a brazier (a type of pan). In the brazier, the brothers had placed shredded wood and straw. Everyone watched as one of the brothers lit the wood and straw. The fire warmed the air, which began filling the balloon. The balloon came to life. It swelled and bucked. And then it rose 6,000 feet (1,829 m) into the air. Air currents carried it about a mile and a half (2 kilometers) before it settled back to earth in a vineyard.

In the fall, the brothers decided to show their invention to King Louis XVI and Queen Marie Antoinette. This time, there were passengers: a sheep, a duck, and a rooster. A huge crowd gathered in front of the royal palace in Versailles. The new balloon rose. Then a great gust of wind took it on a 2-mile (3 km) trip. The balloon landed safely, the animals were fine, and the king and the queen were impressed. A few months later, two Frenchmen went up in a new Montgolfier balloon. They traveled across the city of Paris and remained in the air for about twenty minutes. It was the first human flight in a balloon that wasn't attached to the ground.

Balloons are the oldest form of air transportation humans have created. In modern times, balloons carrying scientific instruments help predict the weather.

On September 19, 1783, thousands of people gathered to watch a sheep, a duck, and a rooster fly in a Montgolfier balloon.

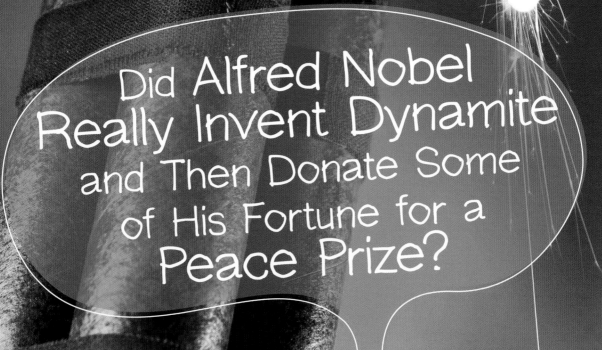

Did Alfred Nobel Really Invent Dynamite and Then Donate Some of His Fortune for a Peace Prize?

YES! In 1866, Alfred Nobel mixed a pale yellow oil called nitroglycerin with a powdery substance called kieselguhr. The result was dynamite. This hard material produces powerful explosions. By the time Nobel died, he owned more than ninety dynamite and ammunition factories. He left instructions for his wealth to be used to award five prizes every year. One is the Nobel Peace Prize.

r Nobel, making explosions came aturally. His father was in the business f making explosives. In 1862, when obel was a young man, he and is father built a factory to produce itroglycerin. It was very dangerous to vork with. In fact, it was so dangerous hat the factory blew up. Nobel's brother Emil died in the explosion.

Nobel wanted to make nitroglycerin safer to work with. When he mixed it with kieselguhr, he found his answer. The resulting dynamite was much safer to transport and easier to use than nitroglycerin.

After Nobel died in 1896, his will was opened. It contained the instructions for using his money to set up the Nobel Prizes. In 1901, the first four prizes were given to people who had made important contributions in physics, chemistry, medicine, and literature. The fifth prize went to a Frenchman and a man from Switzerland who had contributed to world peace.

Alfred Nobel in 1863

Alfred Nobel appears on the medal awarded to Nobel Prize winners.

Did You Know?

No one is sure why Alfred Nobel left his fortune for the Nobel Prizes. But it might have something to do with an incident that occurred after his brother Emil died in the factory explosion. A French newspaper mistakenly reported that it was Alfred who had died. The paper described Alfred as a "merchant of death" because he helped to make ammunition. Nobel could not have been very happy to hear himself described that way. So perhaps he thought the Nobel Prizes would encourage people to remember him more favorably than that French newspaper had!

Is It Possible That Alexander Graham Bell Didn't Invent the Telephone?

YES, IT'S POSSIBLE. Most people give Alexander Graham Bell credit for inventing the telephone. He received a patent for it in 1876. But an inventor named Elisha Gray missed getting a patent for that same invention by only two hours. And he probably designed his version of the telephone first.

Both Bell and Gray gave the patent authorities a sketch of their inventions. Bell's sketch was dated March 9, 1876. Gray's was dated February 11, 1876. But the sketches arrived at the patent office on the same day. What took Gray so long to apply for a patent? He just didn't take his invention seriously enough.

Neither Bell nor Gray had set out to create a telephone. They were trying to make the telegraph system better. Telegraph machines used electrical signals to send messages over wires. While working on the telegraph system in 1874, Elisha Gray made a discovery. He figured out a way to send musical notes over telegraph wires. And he gave demonstrations around the country. He was getting close to being able to send speech over wires. But big businesses didn't see any point in such an invention. They wanted someone to invent a way to send several messages over telegraph wires at once. Gray decided big business might be right. Maybe the telephone would be more like a toy.

Alexander Bell found the idea of sending speech over wires exciting. And he thought such an invention might be useful. In fact, he thought that one day most homes would have telephones, just as most homes had water and gas.

Bell and his assistant, Thomas Watson, worked on Bell's invention day after day. On March 10, 1876, Bell spoke into the phone. And Watson heard him on his receiver in another room. They made history that day. After Bell received the patent, Gray went to court to try to take it away from him. But the court thought Bell deserved to keep the patent.

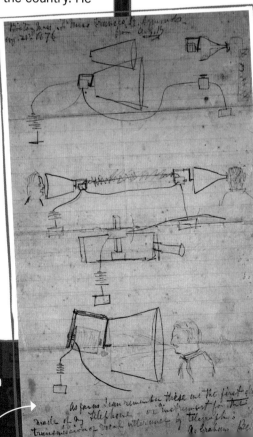

Alexander Graham Bell's original sketch of a telephone from 1876

Did Thomas Edison Invent the First Lightbulb?

NO. But he was the first inventor to design a lightbulb and a large electrical system that worked together. Edison wanted to light up New York City! But first, he needed a good lightbulb.

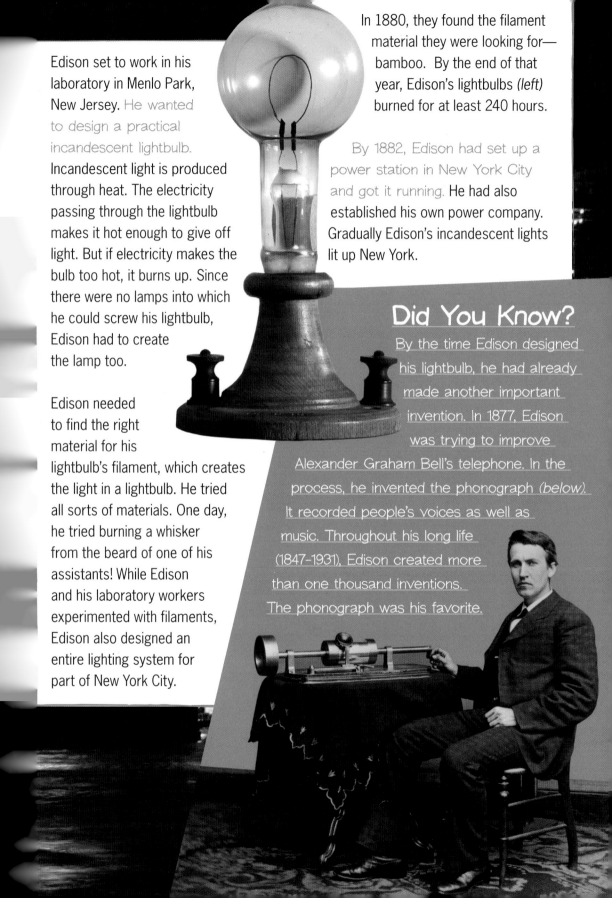

Edison set to work in his laboratory in Menlo Park, New Jersey. He wanted to design a practical incandescent lightbulb. Incandescent light is produced through heat. The electricity passing through the lightbulb makes it hot enough to give off light. But if electricity makes the bulb too hot, it burns up. Since there were no lamps into which he could screw his lightbulb, Edison had to create the lamp too.

Edison needed to find the right material for his lightbulb's filament, which creates the light in a lightbulb. He tried all sorts of materials. One day, he tried burning a whisker from the beard of one of his assistants! While Edison and his laboratory workers experimented with filaments, Edison also designed an entire lighting system for part of New York City.

In 1880, they found the filament material they were looking for—bamboo. By the end of that year, Edison's lightbulbs *(left)* burned for at least 240 hours.

By 1882, Edison had set up a power station in New York City and got it running. He had also established his own power company. Gradually Edison's incandescent lights lit up New York.

Did You Know?

By the time Edison designed his lightbulb, he had already made another important invention. In 1877, Edison was trying to improve Alexander Graham Bell's telephone. In the process, he invented the phonograph *(below)*. It recorded people's voices as well as music. Throughout his long life (1847–1931), Edison created more than one thousand inventions. The phonograph was his favorite.

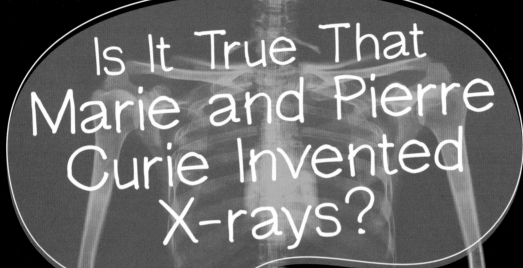

Is It True That Marie and Pierre Curie Invented X-rays?

NOPE. Marie Curie and Pierre Curie, who were married to each other, did not invent X-rays. The Curies discovered radium. Like X-rays, radium proved to be very useful for doctors. They used radium to treat cancer.

So who discovered X-rays? Wilhelm Conrad Roentgen discovered them in his laboratory in 1895. These unusual rays could travel through a person's flesh. In fact, Roentgen discovered how to make a picture of someone's bones with the help of these rays.

A few months after Roentgen made his discovery, a French scientist discovered another type of ray. This ray didn't come out of a laboratory. It occurred in nature. The rays were produced by uranium. Uranium is a metal-like element that can be found in rocks, water, and soil. The French scientist's discovery didn't attract much attention. Most scientists in Europe found Roentgen's X-rays more exciting.

But Marie and Pierre Curie wanted to know more about the uranium rays. So they studied them. And the Curies made some important discoveries. They realized that the atoms (the tiniest particles) in uranium constantly broke down. And when they broke down, they gave off energy in the form of rays. Marie Curie called this behavior of the uranium atoms radioactivity. Uranium was a radioactive element. The Curies realized that other elements were radioactive too. And in 1898, they discovered two new radioactive elements: radium and polonium.

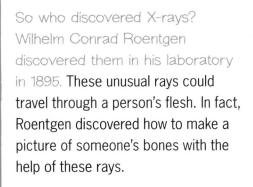

Marie and Pierre Curie in their laboratory in Paris

Did Henry Ford Really Invent the Automobile?

Henry Ford made a major contribution to the long history of the automobile. But he didn't invent automobiles.

The Ford Model T

In 1908, Ford introduced his Model T car. It cost $850, which was inexpensive compared to other cars on the market. A lot of people wanted to buy the Ford Motor Company's Model T. To make enough cars, Ford figured out a way for the company's factory workers to produce his cars more quickly. In 1913, he introduced the moving assembly line.

Ford installed a moving belt in his car factory. As the belt moved along, workers assembled one car part at a time. Before the moving belt arrived in the factory, workers had put together one entire car at a time. The body of the car took more than twelve hours to produce. With the help of the moving assembly line, it took about an hour and a half. Since each car took less time to produce, Ford saved money. And he reduced the price of the Model T. By 1915, he was charging only $290 for it.

Other automobile makers copied Ford's methods. Many more Americans could afford to buy these cheaper cars. The age of the automobile had arrived.

Ford made another change in 1914 that he knew would please his workers. He paid them more than his competitors paid their workers. Each Ford worker earned at least five dollars a day. That was twice what they had earned before.

The First Automobiles

The first automobile was actually a steam-powered carriage. The French engineer Nicolas-Joseph Cugnot built it in 1769. A year later, he built a larger one. It rode on three wheels and traveled at 3 miles (5 km) per hour. Modern cars travel at speeds about 65 miles (105 km) per hour on highways. Although Cugnot's carriage was very slow by modern standards, it caused the first motor vehicle accident. A driver crashed the carriage into a wall, destroying the wall.

Did a Melted Candy Bar Really Inspire Percy L. Spencer to Invent the Microwave Oven?

An early microwave oven

YES! Percy L. Spencer worked as an engineer at the Raytheon Company in Massachusetts. One day, in 1946, Spencer stopped in front of a piece of equipment called a magnetron. He suddenly realized that a candy bar in his pocket was melting. That seemed odd. Like any good inventor, he decided to investigate.

Spencer knew that a magnetron produces microwaves. These energy waves can pass through many materials. But they bounce off metal. For this reason, the U.S. military used Raytheon's magnetrons in radar systems during World War II (1939–1945). The microwaves helped the military find enemy planes and boats.

Spencer thought the microwaves coming from the magnetron might be melting the chocolate. To test this theory, he got some popcorn kernels that had not yet popped. He held a bag of the kernels in front of the magnetron and turned it on. What do you think happened? Right! The kernels popped.

The popcorn and the candy bar had absorbed the magnetron's microwaves. And the microwaves heated the food. Spencer wondered whether microwaves could cook other food besides popcorn. He brought in a tea kettle and made a hole in it. Then he put an egg in the kettle and put the kettle near the magnetron. At exactly the wrong moment, a curious engineer put his face near the kettle hole. The egg exploded, and some of it landed on the engineer's face! Yep, microwaves cooked eggs.

Spencer had discovered a new use for the magnetron—cooking things! In 1953, Raytheon produced the first microwave ovens, which were sold to restaurants and railroads. The huge ovens were 5.5 feet (1.7 m) high and weighed 750 pounds (340 kg). They were much too big for family kitchens. Then, in 1967, Raytheon figured out how to make much smaller microwave ovens. Since then, the microwave oven has become a standard kitchen appliance.

A magnetron, like this one from 1940, gave Spencer the idea for the microwave oven.

Were Early Computers Really the Size of a School Bus?

NO. THEY WERE EVEN BIGGER! IBM finished building one of the earliest computers in 1944. It was almost 51 feet (15 m) long and 8 feet (2.4 m) high. (School buses are usually less than 40 feet, or 12 m, long.) The computer was called the Harvard Mark I.

Two years later came the ENIAC computer. (*ENIAC* was an abbreviation for Electronic Numerical Integrator and Computer.) It was about twice as big as the Harvard Mark I and much faster. It weighed about 60,000 pounds (27,216 kg). Why did it weigh so much? For one thing, the ENIAC contained more than seventeen thousand vacuum tubes. The tubes sent electrical signals through circuits to perform many of the computer's functions. The U.S. government paid for the ENIAC. The military used it to solve mathematical problems in order to build a bomb, design wind tunnels, and even to predict the weather.

These early computers were much too large and expensive for an average consumer. And only trained professionals had the skills to use them. So the computers were mainly at universities and in government departments.

In the 1950s, computers began shrinking. Engineers had developed transistors to take the place of all those vacuum tubes. A transistor is an electronic switch that controls the flow of electricity. It's much smaller than a vacuum tube. New computers with transistors were about the size of a refrigerator.

Then, in 1958, Jack St. Clair Kilby invented the microchip. This tiny chip about the size of a fingernail contained a few transistors. By the early 1980s, computer engineers had figured out how to make a microchip with hundreds of thousands of transistors inside. As a result, computers became smaller, more affordable, and much more powerful.

In 1981, IBM introduced a personal computer *(below)* small enough to sit on someone's desk. Apple Computer brought out the Macintosh three years later. These days, we all depend on computers. Can you imagine life without them?

Were Day-Glo Colors Really Invented Because Someone Hit His Head on a Loading Dock?

YES! In 1933, college student Bob Switzer was working at his summer job. He was trying to climb into a railroad car when he fell and hit his head on a loading dock. Switzer's vision became blurred. His doctor told him to rest in a darkened room. But Switzer found all that downtime boring. So he and his brother Joseph began experimenting with substances that glowed in the light of an ultraviolet lamp. Ultraviolet lamps give off light that is mostly outside the range that people can see.

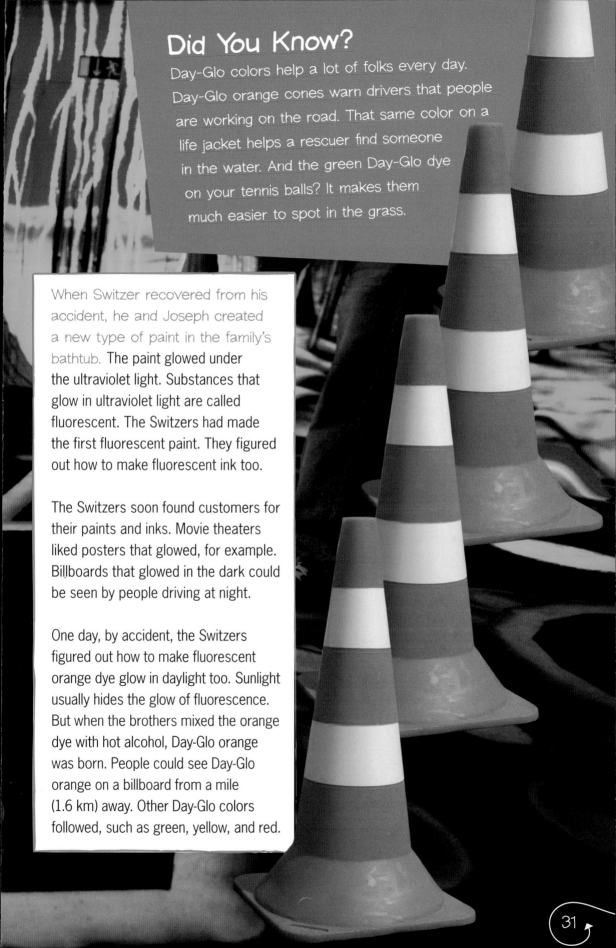

When Switzer recovered from his
accident, he and Joseph created
a new type of paint in the family's
bathtub. The paint glowed under
the ultraviolet light. Substances that
glow in ultraviolet light are called
fluorescent. The Switzers had made
the first fluorescent paint. They figured
out how to make fluorescent ink too.

The Switzers soon found customers for
their paints and inks. Movie theaters
liked posters that glowed, for example.
Billboards that glowed in the dark could
be seen by people driving at night.

One day, by accident, the Switzers
figured out how to make fluorescent
orange dye glow in daylight too. Sunlight
usually hides the glow of fluorescence.
But when the brothers mixed the orange
dye with hot alcohol, Day-Glo orange
was born. People could see Day-Glo
orange on a billboard from a mile
(1.6 km) away. Other Day-Glo colors
followed, such as green, yellow, and red.

Was Frozen Food Really Invented by a Fur Trader?

YES, MORE OR LESS. Clarence Birdseye invented a modern technique for freezing food very quickly. And he did spend several years as a fur trader.

Clarence Birdseye *(left)* invented a machine *(below right)* for quickly freezing packages of food.

In 1912, Birdseye left the United States to work as a fur trader in Labrador, a region in northeastern Canada. Winters are long and very cold there. While Birdseye was in Labrador, he went fishing. It was so cold outside that the fish froze as soon as they came out of the water. Birdseye noticed something interesting. When the frozen fish was thawed and cooked, it tasted delicious. That was true even when the fish had been frozen for months. It was much better than food that had been frozen slowly.

Birdseye realized that the fish kept its flavor and texture because it had frozen so quickly. When food freezes slowly, large ice crystals form. And the ice crystals destroy some of the food's flavor. Birdseye wanted to find a way to freeze food fast—without Labrador's winter weather.

Back in the United States, Birdseye began experimenting. In 1924, he invented a method for quickly freezing food. He cooled two hollow metal plates down to −25°F (−32°C). Then he pressed food packages between the plates. The food inside froze in a matter of minutes.

Soon, Birdseye was selling quick-frozen fish fillets and vegetables. By the 1950s, a lot of Americans had refrigerators with freezers. And they bought plenty of Birdseye's frozen foods.

Did You Know?

Before Birdseye invented his quick-freezing method, food companies had other ways of preserving food. They smoked fish and meat. And they canned fruit and vegetables. But none of these tasted as much like freshly prepared food as Birdeye's quick-frozen foods did.

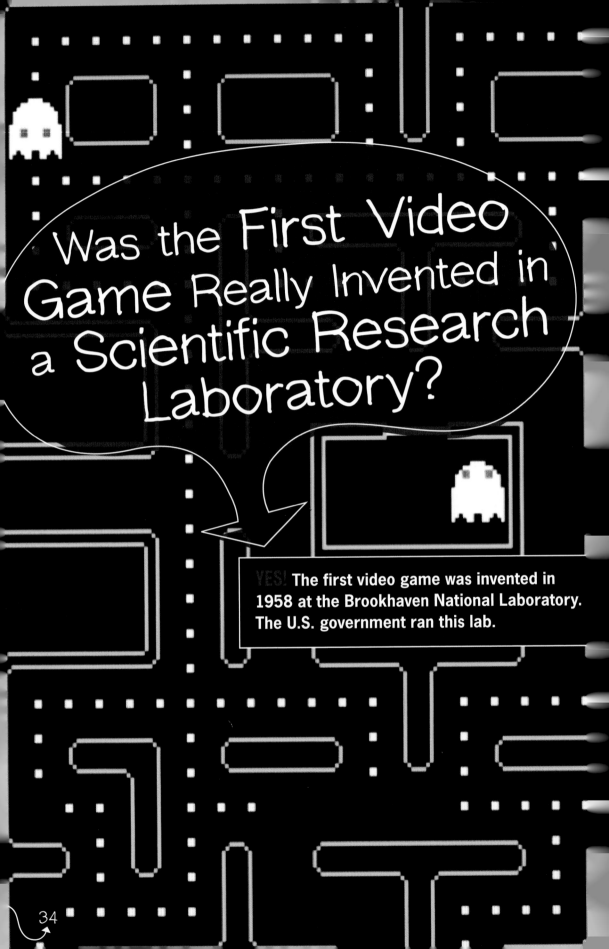

Was the First Video Game Really Invented in a Scientific Research Laboratory?

YES! The first video game was invented in 1958 at the Brookhaven National Laboratory. The U.S. government ran this lab.

The scientists at the lab were doing research on peaceful ways to use nuclear energy. But at the time, Americans worried that the United States might get into a nuclear war with its enemies. So the Brookhaven Lab invited people to visit once a year. The scientists wanted the public to see that nuclear research could be useful and not scary.

William Higinbotham

Two. On the oscilloscope's screen, he created a side view of a tennis court made with glowing green lines. A brightly lit ball bounced from one side of

Tennis for Two was played on a screen just 5 inches (13 centimeters) wide.

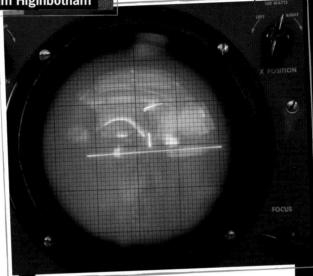

The scientists created exhibits to explain machines such as electronic circuits. But one scientist named William Higinbotham didn't think the exhibits were much fun. Before the visitors day in 1958, he had an idea. He decided to make something adults and kids could play with.

Higinbotham dreamed up a game that two people could play with a computer hooked up to an oscilloscope. An oscilloscope was an instrument with a small screen. It resembled a very old TV set. Higinbotham called his game Tennis for

the net to the other. It left a bright trail of light behind it. Higinbotham made two game controllers with spare parts that lay around the lab. The players used the controllers to serve the ball and hit it back and forth.

On visitors day, Higinbotham's game and lots of scientific exhibits were crowded into a big gym. You could hardly see Higinbotham's game. But the visitors found it immediately. And hundreds of people lined up to play it. Video games have been hard to resist ever since!

Did the U.S. Department of Defense Really Invent the Internet?

NO, BUT THE U.S. DEFENSE DEPARTMENT DESIGNED AN ANCESTOR OF THE INTERNET. It was the first computer network, called ARPANET.

This 1972 map shows the locations of communication centers that ARPANET connected.

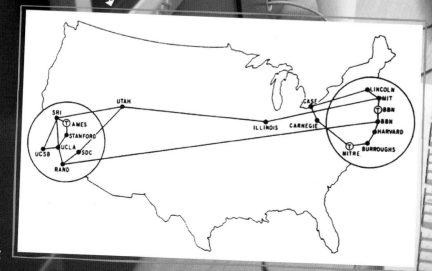

In the early 1960s, the United States was afraid of being attacked by the Union of Soviet Socialist Republics (USSR). This country existed from 1922 to 1991. It was made up of modern-day Russia and other countries. An agency at the Defense Department decided to develop a network of computers in different parts of the United States. If the USSR attacked, the computers in one part of the country might be destroyed. But the other computers in the network could continue working. The agency developing the network was called the Advanced Research Projects Agency (ARPA).

In 1969, ARPA launched its network. ARPANET linked computers at three universities in California and one in Utah. Scientists at these four campuses communicated with one another over the network. By 1981, ARPANET included about two hundred university campuses. But other scientists wanted to join too. So university researchers developed more networks. European researchers developed computer networks too.

People doing research loved being able to share information with others many miles apart. But there was one problem. They could communicate with one another only if they were in the same network. In the 1970s, computer scientists began developing a system so that networks could send one another data. ARPANET adopted this system in 1982. Finally, computer networks could link up with one another. The Internet was born!

The World Wide Web

In 1990, Tim Berners-Lee developed the World Wide Web. The Web makes it easier for people to move around on the Internet and find what they're looking for, whether it's text, images, or sound. The Web is like a well-designed boat that travels easily on a vast ocean of networks.

GLOSSARY

alchemist: an early scientist

ammunition: something that can be fired as a weapon

assembly line: an arrangement for producing a car or another product in stages. A car part, for example, moves from one factory worker to the next until it's finished.

atom: the smallest unit of a substance that still has all of its elements

axis: an imaginary line through the middle of an object, around which the object spins

conduct: to carry energy or allow it to pass through

filament: a fine wire or thread

fluorescent: a word to describe a substance that glows in ultraviolet light

incandescent: glowing from intense heat

kieselguhr: a natural powdery substance used in filters, dynamite, and more

magnetite: a magnetic mineral

microwave: an energy wave that can pass through many solid objects but bounces off metal

nitroglycerin: an explosive that looks like a pale yellow oil

oscilloscope: an electronic instrument with a small screen. Oscilloscopes resembled old TV sets.

patent: a document that gives only the creator of an invention the right to produce and sell that invention for a period of time

phonograph: a machine that plays sounds that have been recorded in the grooves of a record or cylinder

radioactivity: the process by which some elements give off energy in the form of rays

radium: a radioactive element

reflecting telescope: a telescope made with mirrors, which reflect an object

refracting telescope: a telescope made with at least two curved pieces of glass that face in opposite directions

telegraph: a system for sending messages across wires over a long distance

transistor: an electronic switch that controls the flow of electricity

ultraviolet: a type of light that the human eye can't see

uranium: a radioactive element found in rocks, water, and soil. Uranium is used as a source of nuclear energy.

vacuum tube: a sealed glass tube in which electrons act as the main carriers of an electric current

will: written instructions that state what should happen to someone's money and property when he or she dies

SELECTED BIBLIOGRAPHY

Aczel, Amir D. *The Riddle of the Compass: The Invention That Changed the World*. New York: Harcourt, 2001.

Dray, Philip. *Stealing God's Thunder: Benjamin Franklin's Lightning Rod and the Invention of America*. New York: Random House, 2005.

Flatow, Ira. *They All Laughed . . . from Light Bulbs to Lasers: The Fascinating Stories Behind the Great Inventions That Have Changed Our Lives*. New York: HarperPerennial, 1993.

Goddard, Jolyon, ed. *National Geographic Concise History of Science and Invention*. Washington, DC: National Geographic, 2010.

Golden, Frederic, "Who Built the First Computer?" *Time*. March 29, 1999. http://www.time.com/time/magazine/article/0,9171,990596,00.html (November 22, 2010).

Leishman, J. Gordon. "A History of Helicopter Flight." 2000. http://terpconnect.umd.edu/~leishman/Aero/history.html (November 22, 2010).

FURTHER READING

Barton, Chris. *The Day-Glo Brothers: The True Story of Bob and Joe Switzer's Bright Ideas and Brand-New Colors*. Watertown, MA: Charlesbridge, 2009. Read about how the Switzer brothers invented Day-Glo colors in this lively account, illustrated with wonderful drawings in Day-Glo green, orange, and yellow.

Hubblesite
http://hubblesite.org
See the beautiful photos of planets and other heavenly bodies taken from the Hubble telescope, and read about discoveries that scientists have made with its help.

Kops, Deborah. *Were Potato Chips Really Invented by an Angry Chef? And Other Questions about Food*. Minneapolis: Lerner Publications Company, 2011. Have you ever wondered who invented the ice-cream cone? How about fortune cookies or potato chips? Find the answers in this book.

The Lemelson Center for the Study of Invention and Innovation
http://invention.smithsonian.org/centerpieces/sparklab/spark-inventors.html
Read about the fourteen-year-old inventor of the lighted pencil, or click on the Activities and Experiments link for instructions on how to make your own inventions.

The Leonardo Gallery
http://www.museoscienza.org/english/leonardo/galleria
See models of Leonardo da Vinci's wonderful creations, from his air screw helicopter to a printing press.

Marie Curie and the Science of Radioactivity
http://www.aip.org/history/curie/contents.htm
This website on Marie Curie's life and work is packed with information and includes many old photographs.

Thimmesh, Catherine. *Girls Think of Everything: Stories of Ingenious Inventions by Women*. Boston: Houghton Mifflin, 2000. Here you'll find the stories about the women who invented chocolate chip cookies and Snugli baby carriers, and the ten-year-old girl who invented Glo-sheet paper.

INDEX

ACKNOWLEDGMENTS

The images in this book are used with the permission of:
© iStockphoto.com/Gary Blakeley, p. 1; © Steve Vidler/
SuperStock, pp. 2 (left), 14–15; © Science and Society/
SuperStock, pp. 2 (top right, bottom), 4, 11 (inset), 17 (right),
18, 21 (top), 27, 29 (inset); © Ssuaphoto/Dreamstime.com,
pp. 3, 31 (inset); © Erich Lessing/Art Resource, NY, p. 5
(background); © Huntington Library/SuperStock, p. 5 (inset);
© View Stock/Alamy, p. 6; The Granger Collection, New York,
p. 7 (top); © iStockphoto.com/Jeremy Edwards, p. 7 (bottom);
© Trilobite/Dreamstime.com, pp. 8–9; Image courtesy History
of Science Collections, University of Oklahoma Libraries, p. 8
(inset left); © Hulton Archive/Stringer/Getty Images, pp. 8 (inset
right), 24–25, 32 (inset left); © Popperfoto/Getty Images,
p. 9 (inset top); © Dorling Kindersley/Getty Images, p. 9 (inset
bottom); NASA, ESA, K. Kuntz (JHU), F. Bresolin (University
of Hawaii), J. Trauger (Jet Propulsion Lab), J. Mould (NOAO),
Y.-H. Chu (University of Illinois, Urbana), and STScI, pp. 10–11;
© Bettmann/CORBIS, pp. 10 (inset), 21 (bottom), 26; © Paul
Katz/Photolibrary/Getty Images, p. 12; © Hulton Archive/
Getty Images, pp. 13, 17 (left); © Mary Evans Picture Library/
Alamy, p. 14 (inset); Library of Congress, LC-DIG-ppmsca-02472,
p. 15 (inset); © Sam P.S. II/Alamy, p. 16; Library of Congress,
Alexander Graham Bell Family Papers, p. 19; © Nic Cleave
Photography/Alamy, pp. 20–21; © Digital Vision/Getty
Images, pp. 22–23; © Pictorial Press/Alamy, p. 23 (inset);
© iStockphoto.com/Peter Mah, p. 24 (inset); U.S. Army Photo,
pp. 28–29; © Johannes Eisele/AFP/Getty Images, pp. 30–31;
© iStockphoto.com/Elena Aliaga, pp. 32–33; U.S. Patent
1773079, p. 32 (inset right); © Arcadelmages/Alamy, p. 34;
Courtesy of Brookhaven National Laboratory, p. 35 (both);
© Jonathan Storey/Stone/Getty Images, pp. 36–37; © Apic/
Hulton Archive/Getty Images, p. 36 (inset).

Front cover: U.S. Army Photo (ENIAC); © iStockphoto.com/Gary
Blakeley (school bus).

Text copyright © 2011 by Deborah Kops
Illustrations © 2011 by Lerner Publishing Group, Inc.

Lerner Publications Company
A division of Lerner Publishing Group, Inc.
241 First Avenue North
Minneapolis, MN 55401 U.S.A.

Website address: www.lernerbooks.com

Library of Congress Cataloging-in-Publication Data

Kops, Deborah.
    Were early computers really the size of a school bus? :
and other questions about inventions / by Deborah Kops.
    p.   cm. — (Is that a fact?)
    Includes bibliographical references and index.
    ISBN 978–0–7613–6098–8 (lib. bdg. : alk. paper)
    1. Inventions—Miscellanea—Juvenile literature.
    2. Technology—Miscellanea—Juvenile literature.
    3. Science—Miscellanea—Juvenile literature. I. Title.
T48.K595 2011
600—dc22   2010027975

Manufactured in the United States of America
1 – CG – 12/31/10